Your Personal Guide To Motorcycle Wrecks in Kentucky and Indiana
(Second Edition)

AUTHOR, Attorney James "Jim" Desmond
Licensed by the Kentucky and Indiana Bar Associations

Desmond Law Office, PLLC
436 S.7th Street, Ste. 200
Louisville, KY 40203
(502) 609-7657 (My cell phone)
855-REACHMYCELL (TOLL FREE)

WWW.ATTORNEYDESMOND.COM
JDESMONDATTY@YAHOO.COM

Also, the Kentucky and Indiana Bar Association require me to inform you that 1) I will advance the legal costs associated with prosecuting your claim and that these sums do come out of your settlement. So to comply with the rules of the Bar Association, "COURT COSTS AND CASE EXPENSES WILL BE THE RESPONSIBILITY OF THE CLIENT"; 2) However, if I don't recover any money on your behalf, you are not required to reimburse me those costs and; 3) my attorney's fee is charged off the top, on your total recovery.

Also, the Indiana Bar Association requires me tell you that this book is "ADVERTISING MATERIAL."

Further, Desmond Law Office, PLLC, does not presently maintain an office in Indiana.

Fewer Cases—More Time For <u>You</u>

I am "different".

I don't claim to handle every type of personal injury under the sun. I limit my practice to accidents involving automobile, motorcycle, tractor-trailers, as well as accidents involving pedestrians. I especially enjoy the challenge of handling cases involving motorcycle accidents, whether the wreck happens in Kentucky or Indiana. Why?

Motorcycle accidents pose a unique challenge. From my years of handling motorcycle wrecks, I have seen a pattern wherein usually the motorcycle rider suffered severe injuries and the at-fault driver has insufficient insurance overage to cover my client's medical expenses much less their injury claim.

My job, as an attorney, is two-fold. First, I need to recover as much a I can for my client's personal injury claim. This means that I have to determine if there could be multiple layers of liability coverage on the at-fault driver or whether underinsured motorist coverage, whether it is on the motorcycle or a car insurance policy, could apply. Second, I have to do my best to minimize the amount of medical bills and health insurance liens that might have to be paid out of my client's settlement which ultimately, should result in more money in his/her pocket.

This last point illustrates a way in which I believe I am different that the average attorney. Unlike most attorneys, I have an unwritten policy on motorcycle cases wherein my attorney's fee will not be greater than the final amount that my client puts in his pocket for any case settled without litigation.

Let me say that again,

Unlike most attorneys, I have an unwritten policy on motorcycle injury claims wherein my attorney's fee will not be greater than the final amount that my client puts in his pocket for any case settled without litigation.

After all, why would you bother prosecuting your injury claim if the health plan, the hospitals and my law office took all the money you recovered. Personal Injury Claims involve a lot of work on the part of both the attorney and the client. Why put all that work toward something that does not provide you with a benefit?

My job is to maximize the amount I can put in your pocket thereby, hopefully, earning your future referrals of family members and friends. I am sorry but I think it is wrong when law firms walk away with thousands of dollars in attorney's fees but the client walks away with the smallest amount of all involved.

Unfortunately, I can not follow this unwritten policy for cases involving litigation since those cases generally require an attorney to advance anywhere from $1,000 to $10,000 to full prosecute the claim. Nevertheless, you will find I will do my best to be fair as I believe it is a privilege for me to handle your personal injury claim.

Also, the Kentucky and Indiana Bar Association require me to inform you that 1) I will advance the legal costs associated with prosecuting your claim and that these sums do come out of your settlement; 2) if I don't recover any money on your behalf, you are not required to reimburse me those costs and; 3) my attorney's fee is charged off the top, on your total recovery.

MY EXPERIENCE:

I was licensed to practice law in Kentucky in 1993 and in Indiana in 1994. I have defended insurance companies, served as in-house counsel for cab companies and recovered money for large health insurance companies. However, for the last thirteen years, I have done what I enjoy the most. I have represented people injured in car wrecks, motorcycle accidents and tractor-trailer accidents.

Most of my cases are referred to us by former satisfied clients and by other attorneys. My clients know that I enjoy the privilege of handling their case and that I am committed to earning their referrals for their family and friends. My clients are there for me and I want to be there for them.

WHY TRUST ME WITH YOUR MOTORCYCLE WRECK?

Rather arrogantly, let me just say I am good at handling them. I realized a long ago in my career that motorcycle accidents are not just like car accidents. Motorcycles have a special set of statutes that apply just to them. Moreover, unlike most car accidents, most motorcycle accidents tend to involve permanent, long-lasting injuries. Whether it is something as simple as scar or early arthritis in an injured limb, motorcycle accidents present their own set of complexities. Unfortunately, all too often the at-fault driver lacks the insurance coverage to adequately compensate my client for the long-term nature of his or her injuries. A few illustrative cases that I have handled illustrate what I am talking about:

> - I had one case wherein a 19-year-old girl, was a passenger on a motorcycle and lost her leg from knee down. I could only recover $50,000 for her and this was only after months of arguing that an uninsured motorist policy applied.

> - I had another case wherein an Army Officer, an experienced motorcycle rider, was six months shy of retiring from the military and was killed by an elderly man driving a Buick with only $250,000 in insurance coverage. He had served this country for 19.5 years of military service as well as serving in the Iraq War. My client was only in his early 40's and he had a job lined up to act as a security consultant in the Iraq War with an annual six-figure salary. His future lost wages alone were about four times more than what we could recover.

> - I handled another case involving a Ft. Knox soldier who had 15 years of military service and he was discharged because of the injuries sustained in the motor vehicle accident. This solider was hit by a semi-tractor trailer with plenty of insurance coverage. As a result, after extensive litigation and bringing co-counsel into the lawsuit, we recovered $650,000 on his behalf.[1]

---

[1] There is a friend of mine, William Driscoll, who knows significantly more about semi-tractor trailer accidents than I do. As a result, our client got the best of both worlds in that he got my experience with motorcycle accidents and William's experience with semi-tractor trailer accidents. However, my client's attorney fees remained the same as if only one attorney had been involved in the case. William and I just split the attorney's fee that the client had already agreed to with my office.

> ➤ I just recently handled a motorcycle case wherein my client's initial hospital bill was over $22,000 and the at-fault driver was only insured for the state minimum, $25,000 per person. [2] The saving grace on this claim was that we were able to find underinsured motorist coverage, on an automobile insurance policy, that covered my client's injuries while he was riding a motorcycle.

I will discuss below about this last case again later in the book because it illustrates both the need for underinsured motorist coverage and the battle with a health plan to prevent their subrogation/right of reimbursement claim from eating up my client's recovery.

Out of all the sections in this book, I really hope you will take the time to read the sections about insurance coverage because arguably, those are the most important sections. Very simply, when a motorcycle wreck happens, it Is like a photograph is taken. All the insurance coverage that applies is in that photograph and none can be removed from that photograph. As a result, all attorneys, no matter who you hire, are constrained by the motorcycle insurance you purchased before the motorcycle wreck ever occurred.

---

[2] In both Kentucky and Indiana, drivers can carry as little as $25,000 per person of insurance coverage.

THE LAW IS NOT FAIR!

While I might be leading off with one of the more depressing sides of the law, it is also probably one of the most important for you to understand. While the law endeavors to be fair, it is not always fair!

If the law were fair there would be no point in writing this book. For if the law were fair, the at-fault driver would have plenty of money to pay your medical expenses as they are incurred and assist you in getting your motorcycle repaired. He would also be responsible for driving you to every doctor and physical therapy appointment you have until you were back in the same condition you were prior to his negligence that caused this motor vehicle wreck. However, this is not how the law works.

The law allows you to recover one thing, money! That is all the law allows you to recover for your pain and suffering. In fact, there is nothing in the law that can force the at-fault driver to even apologize to you.

My point being that when you read this book, **you will understand a central concept which is you have to protect yourself before the motor vehicle crash or motorcycle wreck happens.** You have to assume that you are going to be hit by a deadbeat that can't keep a steady job at the local grocery store and has $5 to his name. Since Kentucky and Indiana law allow this type of person to operate a motor vehicle lawfully upon our highways as long as their vehicle is insured for the state minimum of $25,000 per person, you have to know what kind of insurance coverage to put on your motorcycle before the wreck happens. Otherwise, every time you go on the road, you are placing at risk your savings, retirement and the possibility that you may not be able to get the proper treatment for your injuries.

Don't gamble! Call me before the car accident even happens if you have questions. My cell phone is 502-609-7657. Better yet, send me a copy of the declarations page from your motorcycle insurance. I will mark it up and send it back to you with my recommendations as to your insurance coverage.

HOW DO I VALUE MY CASE?

You don't listen to your friends when they will tell you that they know of someone who did not get hurt and they recovered $25,0000. While I wish that were the case, it probably isn't. Insurance companies fight before they just hand over money to an injured person. Also, you don't try to use standard formulas like three times your medical expenses. Those formulas existed in the past and are no longer used by insurance carriers. These ways will take you down the wrong road and you may end up in a lawsuit because of false expectations.

Until someone looks at all your medical records, no attorney can really provide you with a value for your case. A case value depends upon a multitude of factors including: amount of property damage; length of treatment; type of treatment; lost wages; medical conditions existing before the accident; liability for the accident; aggravating circumstances such as a drunk driver; insurance company involved and; prior experience with this particular insurance adjuster.

I see many attorneys act like realtors when they first speak to a potential client and promise them the world to sign up the case. Realtors, to obtain a house listing, have no problem using the figures you want to believe your house is worth only to tell you six months later, "Sorry I was wrong and the market changed." I won't do that. I am not going to promise you the moon and let you get your hopes up only to change my story once the first low offer comes in from the insurance carrier.

As an attorney who knows other attorneys with also extensive personal injury practices, I have an advantage that you don't. Many times, without revealing information protected by the attorney-client privilege, will discuss your case with attorney friends of mine so I can get their input as what they believe the case is worth. Basically, I want to make sure that I am accurately valuing your personal injury claim. After all, as an attorney who is always advocating for you, it is not hard to start believing our own hype. I don't want to put you through the rigors of a lawsuit unless I am sure that the case justifies it and the insurance company has incorrectly valued the claim.

If you want an attorney who will give you a straightforward, honest evaluation of your case, I can do that.

LIABILITY! WHO IS AT FAULT IN CAUSING THE MOTORCYCLE WRECK?

The first question for any personal injury claim is who caused the motorcycle crash? We want to gather information about how the car wreck happened immediately. If you are at the scene of an automobile accident, do not hesitate to take your cell phone out and take pictures of the accident scene. Take pictures of everything you can. Obviously, I am not telling you to concentrate on taking photographs and neglect your injuries. Rather, if you or your family members have the means to take pictures of the accident scene, do it. Stories as to how the motorcycle crash happened can change. However, as the old saying goes, a picture is worth a thousand words.

Also, you need to understand that the perception the public still has of motorcycle riders is that they are reckless drivers that speed and cut through traffic. As soon at the motorcycle crash happens, you need to gather evidence to fight that misconceived idea. One of the best ways to establish the other driver was at fault is to take pictures of the accident scene. Further, take pictures of your bruises and scrapes. Insurance companies deal with hundreds of personal injury claims every day. You want to do everything you can to show that your personal injury claim is not their typical claim for pain and suffering.

Also, if liability for the accident is disputed, we can have an expert, known as an accident reconstructionist, view the photos taken by you, your family, the police department as well as your testimony. This accident reconstructionist can provide us with a report as to his expert conclusions as to how the motorcycle crash occurred. We may then choose to furnish this report to the insurance companies in an effort to show them that we can put their driver at fault for the motorcycle wreck. This may very well give us the opportunity to resolve your case without the need for litigation.

An accident reconstructionist can be very expensive so the injuries from the motorcycle wreck have to justify the expense. However, if we move quickly and/or preserve the evidence, we have a better chance that such an expert can help us with a solid opinion as to how the accident happened.

IF YOU THINK LIABLITY IS GOING TO BE DISPUTED, DO NOT WAIT TO SEEK LEGAL ADVICE!

I have handled enough motorcycle accidents to know that most people are dealing with issues involving surgery, broken bones, medical bills and lost wages as soon as they motorcycle wreck occurs. As a result, victims of a motorcycle accident are not thinking about hiring an attorney. While this is understandable, I want you to understand a big problem that can arise from you waiting to seek legal advice. Simply put, we need to preserve as much evidence as possible and get prepared for the possibility that your case may go to trial several years from now.

I recently to you the idea of using an accident reconstructionist. These experts tend to be retired police officers with extensive training in regard to physics, biomechanics and how those sciences relate to a motor vehicle crash. These folks don't come cheap! The last time I used one my firm had to advance $7,000 for his investigation and his report. However, without his report, we had no case at all since the majority of fault seemed to rest with the motorcycle operator whom I was representing.

My point being that while there is still evidence on the roadway and while the vehicles can still be located, we want to consider whether an accident reconstructionist can help us and is worth the expense. Such an expert can give me an informal opinion as to whether he believes we can prove the other driver was at fault in causing the motorcycle wreck. Granted, even such an informal investigation can cost more than $1,000 so we cannot do it for every case. However, if the injuries justify the expense and you contact my office quickly, we at least have the opportunity to see what evidence, if any, we can gather from the roadway that the investigating officer may have missed.

All personal injury cases are different but I previously I handled a case for an automobile accident that occurred on a small back road in Indiana. The automobile accident occurred on a two-lane road and the question was who crossed the center-line thereby causing a head-on collision. My client was a newly licensed driver who only had obtained her driver's license maybe six months before the car wreck occurred. Since the other driver was an older lady who had her driver's license for many years, everyone's first impression was that my young driver was the one who crossed the center-line. Luckily, my client's mother contacted me shortly after the accident and we were able to send an accident reconstructionist to the accident scene. Based upon the information my accident reconstructionist provided me in a report, I was able to convince the insurance company for the elder lady that she was completely at fault for the car wreck. I recall that we were able to recover the policy limits for my client. Moreover, it should be noted that the insurance company had hired an accident reconstructionist of their own. The insurance company's expert reviewed our report and agreed with everything contained therein. This is a wonderful example of how moving quickly can make all the difference in showing who was at fault in causing the motorcycle crash. While every case may not warrant the use of an accident reconstructionist, moving quickly gives us the opportunity to enlist the help of such an expert when it is called for.

COMPARATIVE FAULT. WHAT DO I HAVE TO SHOW IN KENTUCKY OR INDIANA?

Kentucky is a pure comparative fault state. In essence, this means that a jury could find you were 95% at fault for causing a motorcycle wreck and yet, you would still be allowed to recover 5% of your damages. It does not matter what percentage you use as long as the apportionment of fault, between the drivers, adds up to 100%. In other words, as long as a jury does not find you 100% at fault for causing a motorcycle crash, you can recover some of your damages.

In contrast, Indiana is a modified comparative fault state. This means that you cannot recover any of your damages unless the other driver bore the majority of fault for the motorcycle crash. In other words, if a jury says you are 50% or more at fault in causing the motorcycle crash, you would not be allowed to recover any of your damages. In Indiana, you have to be 49% or less at fault in causing the motorcycle wreck or you cannot recover any of your damages.

As a result, the first question we have to look at is can we and how do we prove fault by the other driver? The first step is to take a look at the police report and see what it says. Also, does the police report list any witnesses or do we know of any witnesses not listed on the police report? Chances are, unless liability is very clear, we may want to get written or recorded statements from these witnesses right away. If it looks like fault may be disputed, we may want to hire an accident reconstructionist as we talked about above. Also, who said what after the accident occurred and were there any surveillance cameras that may have caught the motorcycle wreck on film?

I AM NOT AT FAULT IN CAUSING THE MOTORCYCLE WRECK. WHAT DO I DO NEXT?

My first concern with every motorcycle accident I handle is *"How am I going to get my client's medical expenses paid?"* Very simply, healthcare is not cheap and in most cases involving motorcycle accidents, the medical bills tend to be very high. For example, the helicopters that fly people from the accident scene to the trauma center tend to be an average cost of about $25,000.

When I first sign up a motorcycle case, I look for insurance on the other driver and I want to know how much. At the same time, I will immediately request the medical records and bills for my client's EMS and Hospital stay. This is because very soon after we know which carrier the at-fault driver is insured with, I want to be able to stress to insurance company that this is not the typical personal injury claim. One of the best ways to do that is to hit them early with medical records and bills demonstrating that your injury is more severe, with more medical expenses, than may they may expect in a typical motor vehicle accident.

My next step is to find a way to get your medical bills paid if there is one. Ideally, you have health insurance that will cover these bills. I am also looking for med-pay coverage or no-fault coverage.[3]

If this kind of insurance coverage is not present, we might have to consider giving your doctor a lien on your personal injury claim. This means that we both agree that the doctor's charges are paid before you receive any funds from your personal injury claim. While this is not ideal, it may be are only way of getting you the treatment you need for your injuries.

Next, I usually turn my attention back to the motorcycle and automobile policies you own. This time, I am looking for uninsured and underinsured motorist coverage. Basically, I am hoping your own motorcycle or automobile insurance will provide us with a fallback in case this other driver has no insurance or very little insurance.

---

[3] These types of coverage are discussed below.

Once I have a first idea as to these types of coverage, I will meet with my client again so as to figure out my game plan and my expectations as to where we can succeed on his/her personal injury claim. Of course, the game plan can change as more facts are learned about the motorcycle accident but, I think it is important that my client understand the legal process and the pitfalls in regard to the same.

A BRIEF DESCRIPTION OF KENTUCKY MOTORCYCLE LAWS

HOW LONG DO I HAVE TO FILE A PERSONAL INJURY CLAIM FROM MOTORCYCLE ACCIDENT?

This question is referring to the Statute of Limitations. In Kentucky, most personal injury claims have a one-year statute of limitations. This time limit is contained in KRS 413.135. However, for motor vehicle accidents, Kentucky law says that the statute of limitations is two-years from the date of the accident or two-years from the date of the last no-fault payment. [4] The Kentucky statute of limitations for motor vehicle accidents is contained in KRS 304.39-230.

The Statute of Limitations varies according to the state law that applies as well as the type of case we are dealing with. In Kentucky and Indiana both, the statute of limitations for a motorcycle accident is two years from the date of the accident.[5] This means that suit must be filed, with the proper court, within two years of the date of the accident or the claim is barred like it never existed.

Now, forget everything I just said just above and listen to this: **YOU ARE BUILDING YOUR PERSONAL INJURY CLAIM FROM THE MOMENT THE MOTOR VEHICLE ACCIDENT HAPPENS!**

The way the system works is that your personal injury claim lives and dies on the information contained in your medical records. As a result, if you don't go seek treatment for the first four weeks following a motor vehicle accident, it looks like you were not hurting for those four weeks!

So, yes, from a legal standpoint, you have time to resolve your personal injury claim. However, from a practical standpoint, your case lives and dies on the content of your medical records. Please note that I

---

[4] With motorcycle accidents, you generally do not see no-fault coverage. As a result, you should assume that the statute of limitations is two years from the date of the accident to be safe.

[5] In Kentucky, the statute of limitations is actually two years from the date of the accident or two years from the date of the last no-fault payment. Nevertheless, I would hope you would contact me to discus this issue rather than take the chance that you have applied the wrong statute of limitations.

am not telling you to seek medical treatment when you don't need it. I am telling you to seek medical treatment if you need it and don't wait weeks thinking that the injuries will resolve by themselves. If you don't know how your medical treatment is going to be paid for, call my cell phone, (502) 609 – 7657, and I will be happy to discuss it with you at no charge.

One of the hardest cases for me to win is where someone does not seek treatment for the first four weeks after a motor vehicle accident. In this scenario, I have the additional burden of showing that your injury was caused by this motor vehicle accident and no other accident (e.g. slip and fall) happened from the time of the accident until your first treatment. If you are in fact hurting from a motor vehicle accident, get the medical treatment you need as further delay only hinders the prosecution of your personal injury claim.

DOES KENTUCKY LAW REQUIRE A HELMET WHEN I RIDE MY MOTORCYCLE?

Kentucky law does not require all riders to use a helmet. The statute is KRS 189.285. If you're over 21 and have had your operator's license for more than a year, you may operate your motorcycle without a helmet. This is true whether you are a passenger or the operator of the motorcycle.

However, if you are under 21 and have had your license for less than a year, you must wear a helmet. Passengers must be over 21 to ride without a helmet.

WHAT DO I NEED TO LAWFULLY OPERATE A MOTORCYCLE IN KENTUCKY?

KRS 189.285 says that you have to have:
1) a valid motorcycle operator's license;
2) an eye protective device and;
3) a rear-view mirror on the motorcycle.

DO I NEED A MOTORCYCLE OPERATOR'S LICENSE IN KENTUCKY?

Yes. Your motorcycle is a motor vehicle and unless you are operating your bike only a private property, you need a motorcycle operator's license.

I ONLY HAVE AN INSTRUCTION PERMIT. CAN I LET A PASSENGER RIDE ON MY MOTORCYCLE?

No. Kentucky law requires you to have a motorcycle operator's license before you can lawfully carry a passenger.

I WANT TO LEARN HOW TO RIDE A MOTORCYCLE. WHERE DO I BEGIN?

The Kentucky Motorcycle Safety Program has schools set up throughout the Commonwealth. They can be contacted at 800-396-3234.

WHAT IS THE DIFFERENCE BETWEEN A MOTORCYCLE AND A MOPED?

According to KRS 189.285, a moped has less than 50 cubic centimeters of cylinder capacity. Anything in excess of that is considered a motorcycle.

HOW MUCH INSURANCE DO I NEED ON MY MOTORCYCLE TO GET IT LICENSED?

The minimum amount of insurance you need on your motorcycle is governed by KRS 304.39-110. This statute says you need liability insurance coverage of at least $25,000 per person, $50,000 per accident and $10,000 in property damage. You can have one insurance policy with a single limit of $60,000 to comply with these requirements.

I strongly recommend that you have more insurance than the minimums prescribed by KRS 304.39-110. Whatever you do, please don't stop reading this book at this point. Please read below to discover why the Kentucky or Indiana statutes put you at risk for becoming bankrupt from a motorcycle accident.

WHAT IF THE INSURANCE COMPANY FOR MY MOTORCYCLE DOES NOT OFFER THE NO-FAULT COVERAGE, UNINSURED MOTORIST AND UNDERINSURED MOTORIST COVERAGE?

The statute is KRS 304.39-040(3). If your insurance company sells motorcycle insurance within the Commonwealth of Kentucky, they are required to at least offer you the kind of insurance coverage we are talking about.

MY MOTORCYCLE INSURANCE POLICY SAYS I HAVE "PEDESTRIAN PIP". DOES THIS MEAN I AM PROTECTED?

No. Kentucky is what is referred to as a no-fault state. For accidents involving pedestrians, this means that the vehicle that hits the pedestrian is responsible for that pedestrian's medical expenses up to $10,000. For motorcycles, Pedestrian PIP is referring to this concept. You are basically paying for pip coverage for the pedestrian you hit with your motorcycle. This kind of PIP coverage does not in any way protect you or your passenger.

I WAS IN A MOTORCYCLE ACCIDENT AND MY INSURANCE COMPANY IS NOW SAYING THEY DON'T OWE MY MEDICAL BILLS OR LOST WAGES. WHAT ARE THEY TALKING ABOUT?

Kentucky is a no-fault state. In essence, this means that the insurance company for the vehicle you are riding in is responsible for your medical bills and lost wages up to $10,000.[6] So if you are in my car and we are hit by a drunk driver while waiting for a stoplight to change, my insurance company owes you $10,000 of medical expense and lost wage coverage. It does not matter that I was not at fault in causing the accident. They have to pay the no-

---

[6] No fault benefits include other elements not discussed herein.

fault benefits and try to recover them from the drunk driver's insurance company.

Kentucky law says in exchange for this right, you give up the right to recover the first $10,000 in medical expenses and lost wages and it becomes the right of the insurance carrier, a.k.a. the PIP carrier. The statute is KRS 304.39-060. This statute says if there is no PIP carrier, your still lose the right to recover the first $10,000 in medical expenses and lost wages. In essence, the statute is punishing you for not having your vehicle properly insured.

As unfair as it is, Kentucky law acts like a motorcycle operator is an uninsured driver. As a motorcycle operator or a motorcycle passenger, Kentucky law says you are not entitled to PIP insurance unless you specifically purchased it for your motorcycle. See KRS 304.39-040(4). Most motorcyclists don't purchase PIP coverage as it is expensive insurance.

As a result, if you are riding a motorcycle and you did not purchase PIP coverage, KRS 304.39.060 controls. This statute, as discussed above, says it is not your right but the right of the PIP carrier to recover the first $10,000 in medical expenses and lost wages. In other words, even though your motorcycle is lawfully insured, Kentucky law is going to penalize you as soon as you get on that motorcycle, treat you like your motorcycle was completely uninsured and not allow you to recover the first $10,000 of your medical expenses and/or lost wages.[7]

AS A MOTORCYCLE OPERATOR, CAN I GET AROUND THIS $10,000 PENALTY.

Kentucky law does allow you to reject your no-fault benefits. The rejection has to be filed with the Kentucky Department of Insurance and by filing it, you can recover the first $10,000 in medical expenses and lost wages from the insurance company for the at-fault driver. However, if you do this, only file a rejection for your motorcycle and make sure you have health insurance to cover

---

[7] There are arguments under the statutes that contradict this interpretation. However, in my experience, these arguments have not been successful.

your medical expenses. Otherwise, you are taking a big gamble as to whether we can get your medical bills paid or get you the medical treatment you need.

CAN A PASSENGER ON A MOTORCYCLE RECOVER HER MEDICAL EXPENSES?

Yes. Attorneys too often overlook this exception. KRS 304.39-040 says a passenger on a motorcycle is not entitled to PIP coverage. However, KRS 304.39-060(2)(c) says a passenger can recover her medical expenses and lost wages in tort. In other words, your passenger has a personal injury claim for the full amount of their medical bills against the at-fault driver.

HOW DO I FIND OUT MORE ABOUT KENTUCKY MOTORCYCLE LAW?

Motor vehicle accidents in Kentucky are controlled by the Kentucky Motor Vehicle Reparations Act. That Act can be found at section 304.39 et seq. of the Kentucky Revised Statutes.

A BRIEF DESCRIPTION OF INDIANA MOTORCYCLE LAW

HOW DOES INDIANA DEFINE A MOTORCYCLE?

Indiana statutes define a motorcycle as "a motor vehicle with motive power having a seat or saddle for the use of the rider and designed to travel on not more than three (3) wheels in contact with the ground. The term does not include a farm tractor or a motorized bicycle." That definition comes form Indiana Code 9-13-2-108.

DO I HAVE A MOTORCYCLE OR MOPED ACCORDING TO INDIANA LAW?

Indiana law says over 50 CC's, it is a motorcycle. Under 50 CC's, it is a moped. The specific statute is **IC 9-13-2-109 which says**:

> *"Motorized bicycle" means a two (2) or three (3) wheeled vehicle that is propelled by an internal combustion engine or a battery powered motor, and if powered by an internal combustion engine, has the following: 1) An engine rating of not more than two (2) horsepower and a cylinder capacity not exceeding fifty (50) cubic centimeters. (2) An automatic transmission. 3) A maximum design speed of not more than twenty-five (25) miles per hour on a flat surface. The term does not include an electric personal assistive mobility.*

DO I NEED A HELMET TO RIDE A MOTORCYCLE IN INDIANA?

No. If you are over 18, you don't need a helmet. If you are under 18, yes you have to wear a helmet that has a protective face shield. The specific statute is IC 9-19-7 and it states:

IC 9-19-7-1 Minors; protective headgear and face shields Sec. 1. An individual less than eighteen (18) years of age who is operating or riding on a motorcycle on the streets or highways shall do the following: (1) Wear protective headgear meeting the minimum standards set by the bureau. (2) Wear protective glasses, goggles, or transparent face shields.

WHAT OTHER EQUIPMENT DO I NEED TO RIDE A MOTORCYCLE IN INDIANA?

IC 9-19-7-2 Handlebars; brakes; footrests; lamps and reflectors Sec. 2. (a) Except as provided in subsection (b), a motorcycle operated on the streets or highways by a resident of Indiana must meet the following requirements: (1) Be equipped with handlebars that rise not more than fifteen (15) inches above the level of the driver's seat or saddle, when occupied. (2) Be equipped with brakes in good working order on both front and rear wheels. (3) Be equipped with footrests or pegs for both operator and passenger. (4) Be equipped with lamps and reflectors meeting the standards of the United States Department of Transportation. (b) A motorcycle manufactured before January 1, 1956, is not required to be equipped with lamps and other illuminating devices under subsection (a) if the motorcycle is not operated at the times when lighted head lamps and other illuminating devices are required under IC 9-21-7-2.

IC 9-19-7-2.5 Rear view mirrors; speedometers; turn signals Sec. 2.5. A motorcycle manufactured before January 1, 1956, is not required to be equipped with the following devices: (1) A rear view mirror. (2) A speedometer. (3) Mechanical or electric turn signals.

DOES INDIANA LAW PENALIZE ME FOR RIDING A MOTORCYCLE?

No. Unlike Kentucky law, Indiana allows a motorcyclist to recover the full amount of their medical expenses from the at-fault driver.

HOW LONG DO I HAVE TO FILE A PERSONAL INJURY CLAIM FROM A MOTORCYCLE WRECK OCCURRING IN INDIANA?

The Statute of Limitations for a motorcycle accident happening in Indiana is two years from the date of the accident. Unlike Kentucky, there is no way to extend this time limit. The relevant statute is Indiana Code 34-11-2-4.

HOW DOES A MOTORCYCLE RIDER GET THEIR MEDICAL BILLS PAID FOR IN INDIANA?

In Indiana, settlements are inclusive of the medical expenses and liens. As a result, the at-fault carrier is legally responsible for your medical bills in Indiana, assuming you can show that they were at fault in causing the motorcycle crash and they have enough insurance coverage to pay your medical expenses.

However, the at-fault driver is not going to settle any part of your claim or pay any part of your medical expenses until they can resolve your entire personal injury claim. As a result, if you were injured in the motorcycle accident, you have to use either med-pay coverage or your health insurance to pay for your medical bills. If you don't have either, then we have to do the following: 1) try to get a doctor to treat you on the condition that he will be paid out of your settlement and; 2) try to negotiate down your medical bills to put more money in your pocket from your settlement.

Of course, the big issue may not be how we are going to get your medical bills paid but rather, how are we going to get you the treatment you need?

DOES INDIANA OFFER MOTORCYCLE SAFETY COURSES?

Yes, if you contact the Indiana Bureau of Motor Vehicles, they can provide you with a listing of the facilities authorized to provide this course.

WHAT ABOUT UNDERINSURED MOTORIST AND UNDERINSURED MOTORIST COVERAGE FOR A MOTORCYCLE ACCIDENT IN INDIANA?

Indiana plays a lousy trick in regard to this kind of coverage. Basically, there is an offset. You can only recover underinsured motorist benefits to the extent that the other driver has less liability insurance than you have underinsured motorist coverage.

For example, If the at-fault driver has $100,000 of liability coverage and you have a $250,000 policy of underinsured motorist coverage, you can only recover a total of $250,000 between all the parties involved. In other words, the underinsured motorist carrier gets to deduct the benefits it owes you to the extent you recovered from the at-fault driver's insurance company. So in this example, the liability carrier pays $100,000 and the underinsured motorist carrier pays another $150,000. So even though you should be able to recover a total of $350,000 since you purchased a $250,000 underinsured motorist policy, Indiana law only lets you recover a total of $250,000. Kentucky law is the exact opposite in that you could recover a total of $350,000, ($100,000 + $250,000) in the above example.

So if your motorcycle is registered in Indiana, I would suggest you have $250,000 or more of underinsured motorist coverage. This is because I see a fair number of insurance policies from Indiana having liability coverage of $100,000. However, if the other driver is insured for $100,000 and you have $100,000 of underinsured motorist coverage, you don't have an underinsured motorist claim. Basically, $100,000 minus $100,000 equals zero. As a result, you can recover $100,000 from the liability carrier and $0 from your own company as underinsured motorist benefits. In

Kentucky, it would be the opposite. You could recover $100,000 from the liability coverage and $100,000 from the underinsured motorist carrier for a total of $200,000.

SO WHAT HAPPENS IF I DRIVE MY MOTORCYCLE OUTSIDE THE STATE IT INSURED IN?

This can actually be a very complicated question that could take an entire book by itself to answer. This area of the law is known as Conflicts of Law and it addresses when a court is going to apply its own law versus the law of another state. However, as a general rule, the answer is that the insurance coverage you buy in your state follows you to other states and that insurance policy is controlled by the law of the state it was issued.

So if you are riding your motorcycle from your home in Kentucky through Indiana, the insurance coverage you purchased in Kentucky still applies for the motorcycle wreck that happened in Indiana. While Indiana law may control the law in regard to the motorcycle wreck, Kentucky law, in regard to your motorcycle insurance policy, should still control.

This is a complicated area of the law and I would encourage you to call me if you think your case presents a Conflicts of Law Issue. However, you should know this: Purchase the insurance coverage you need to protect you and your family and it should follow you to any other state you travel in.

CAN THE DESMOND LAW OFFICE, PLLC, HELP IF MY MOTORCYCLE WRECK HAPPENED OUTSIDE OF KENTUCKY OR INDIANA?

I am only licensed to practice law in Kentucky and Indiana. As a result, if your car wreck or motorcycle accident happened in another state, I will have to refer you to local counsel for that state to handle your case. However, I still want you to call me as I am not giving to give you another attorney's name unless I would let him handle a personal injury claim for me, personally.

I might decide to co-counsel your case with this other attorney but that decision depends upon the circumstances of each case. Regardless, I will use my resources to try and find you someone whom you can trust. I will do my best to find you an attorney who can provide you with competent legal services and who other attorneys recommend.

Don't just trust your personal injury claim to anyone. Make sure it is someone whom other attorneys respect and who would allow them to handle a claim for their own family members.

WHOM SHOULD I NOT TRUST ABOUT MY MOTORCYCLE ACCIDENT?

The simple answer is anyone you don't know. Nowadays, when a motor vehicle accident happens, people will show up at the scene or call you as they found your name on the police report. They will try to act like they have your best interests in mind and what to help you find the right doctor or that your insurance company wants you to go see this particular doctor. I call these people "bird-doggers" as their real intent is to get you connected with an attorney or a chiropractor for their own profit. They also may promise to loan you money against your case. Hang up the phone and walk away from them!

Make sure you know with whom you are dealing. If they say they represent an insurance company, make them prove it. You want your attorney to have your best interests in mind and no one else's. These bird-doggers are claiming to help you are doing so only because they get paid to get you to a certain doctor or lawyer. Avoid them at all costs! While I may like to deal with certain doctor offices, I make it very clear to all the doctors that you are my client and my loyalty runs to you. You are my client and according to the rules of law, I must always act in your best interests. Make sure that anyone who is working on your behalf understands the importance of that statement.

MOTORCYCLE INSURANCE
MAKE SURE YOU HAVE THE RIGHT KIND OF COVERAGE BEFOR YOU GET ON THE BIKE!

Did you notice that the font just above this sentence is about twice the font size for the rest of this book? Why? Because that is the one thing above all else that I want to make sure you do!

When a motorcycle crash happens, it is like a photograph is taken. All the insurance coverage applicable at that minute the photograph is taken stays in that photograph. However, just as no one can remove that motorcycle insurance from the photograph, no one can add insurance coverage to that photograph either. This is why you can change motorcycle or car insurance the day after an accident and the company at the time of the accident, still has responsibility for handling the claim.

You may notice that I used the photograph example for a second-time. Why? Because it is so important that you understand it! The advice I am giving you about no-fault insurance, med-pay benefits, uninsured motorist coverage or underinsured motorist coverage applies no matter who your attorney is! Even if you decide to handle your injury claim on your own, the material about insurance coverage is great advice that applies to car wrecks, automobile accidents and motorcycle wrecks in both Kentucky and Indiana. Also, if you live outside Indiana or Kentucky, your state still has some kind of equivalent type of insurance coverage. Now that you know what it is, go to your insurance agent and buy the kind of insurance you need to protect your family before the accident happens.

Let me be clear about something. I hope you never need the advice I am giving you in this book. I tell all my clients *"No offense but considering the kind of work I do, I hope to never see you again!"* I am not trying to offend them and they are welcome to call me whenever they need me. Nevertheless, I hope that this will be their last motor vehicle accident. Granted, I am giving you advice that is designed to protect you in the event of the really bad motor vehicle accident. Most motor vehicles accidents do not involve surgeries and hospital stays. I don't deny that. I just want yours to be a personal injury case wherein we recovered the full value of your claim and not an amount you were forced to accept. Do your research before the motor vehicle accident and give me, or whomever you hire as an attorney, a means to compensate you for the actual value of your personal injury claim.

SO WHAT INSURANCE DO YOU, ATTORNEY JIM DESMOND, AS A AN EXPERIERNED, PERSONAL INJURY ATTORNEY, RECOMMEND THAT I HAVE?

I tell all the clients of the Desmond Law Office, whether they are driving a motorcycle or car, to carry at least the following insurance coverage:

1) Underinsured Motorist Coverage of at least $100,000 per person;
2) Underinsured Motorist Coverage of at least $100,000 per person and;
3) No-fault, Med-pay or PIP coverage of at least $30,000 per person.

However, if you can afford more insurance coverage than this, buy it! Just make sure you have these three kinds of insurance coverage on your motorcycle.

HOW MUCH INSURANCE COVERAGE DOES JAMES DESMOND HAVE?

I tell you this only so you know I practice what I preach. I have two children and to make sure that they are protected, I have $500,000 of uninsured motorist and $500,000 of underinsured motorist coverage on my automobile insurance policy. I also have $30,000 of no-fault coverage but for reasons discussed below, I expect I will be raising that shortly.

DIVORCED PARENTS AND CAR INSURANCE.

For divorced parents, I want to digress just for a minute because this issue can also apply to motorcycle wrecks or motor vehicle accidents involving scooters. When I first got divorced, my children spent an equal amount of time at my house and my ex-spouse's home. As a result, I sent a letter to my insurance company confirming my interpretation of the insurance policy.

I interpreted my insurance policy so that my children, even if they were riding in my ex-spouse's car, could make a claim for uninsured motorist benefits or uninsured motorist benefits. If they were in a car wreck while staying with my ex-spouse, my children had insurance coverage as a resident relative of my household even though my vehicles were not involved in the motor vehicle accident. My insurance company agreed with my reasoning and sent me a letter confirming my interpretation.

Take this example and apply it to motorcycle law. You need to understand that a motorcycle operator may have insurance coverage through an insurance policy issued to one of their relatives or someone living in the same household as them. This can be crucially important to investigate for a motorcycle accident because the medical bills, without considering your other damages, may exceed the insurance coverage on the at-fault driver. Further, most people don't know they are supposed to put underinsured motorist coverage on their motorcycle insurance policy or look for it when a motorcycle accident occurs. This is why I always say that part of my job as an attorney is to be a Fisherman. I have to know the law well enough to "fish" for other insurance coverage that may apply. The last thing I want to do is walk away from money that could be collected on your behalf.

In one of the cases I described above, I mentioned a young lady who lost part of her leg in a motorcycle wreck. She was a passenger on the motorcycle and the motorcycle operator had no insurance coverage of any kind. The only way we ultimately recovered anything for her was that we were able to make an argument that she lived part-time with her father and fell under his uninsured motorist coverage as a resident relative of the household. Without this argument, we would have recovered nothing.

On this issue, don't guess! Let me look into it and see if I can track down other insurance coverage that may apply. This is not a simple issue that can be addressed easily. Let's make sure it is done right.

MY INSURANCE POLICY SAYS I HAVE 25,000/50,000/10,000 OF LIABILITY COVERAGE. WHAT DOES THIS MEAN?

Before discussing the types of insurance coverage, let's discuss how to read a motorcycle insurance policy. In the example above, the first number refers to what anyone person can recover. So if someone kills you in a motorcycle accident while driving a 1980 Chevrolet insured for the state minimum in Kentucky and Indiana of $25,000 per person, their insurance company is only going to be responsible for $25,000 of your damages. It does not matter whether you worked at McDonald's making minimum wage or were a brilliant hand surgeon. In the instance I described, the insurance company for this at-fault driver is going to say sorry for your luck and if you want any more than this $25,000, you can sue the at-fault driver personally and try to collect against any assets he might own.

Now let me explain something to you. In very, very rare circumstances is an attorney willing to sue an at-fault driver over and above his insurance policy. Why? Because chances are the at-fault driver has nothing to collect. When you file a lawsuit you are trying to obtain a judgment against that person. A judgment is a piece of paper that says they owe you money, nothing more. If someone has a house that you can foreclose or a bank account you can garnish, then it can be powerful means of collecting the money they owe you. On the other hand, if someone is driving around with just $25,000 in insurance coverage, chances are they have nothing from which to collect that judgment. If someone has a lot of assets, they have a lot of insurance coverage to protect those assets. If they have just enough insurance coverage to lawfully operate a motor vehicle on the road, chances are they don't own a house and they are just getting by each week on their salary. Further, if your judgment is just one of several that they have against them, they are not going to be intimidated by your collections efforts.[8]

In the instance above, the second number, $50,000, refers to the maximum the insurance carrier for the at-fault driver will pay out no matter how many people are injured. So if you are riding your motorcycle, as part of a club, and your wife is a passenger on your bike, it means that if even there were 100 motorcyclists injured by this Chevrolet, the insurance carrier for the at-fault driver is still only responsible for $50,000.

To make matters worse, the situation I just described is called an interpleader. In essence, it means that the insurance carrier cannot settle one of the personal injury claims unless it can settle all of them for the $50,000 or less. So usually the insurance carrier will file a lawsuit, known as an interpleader. Interpleader is a cause of action wherein the insurance company is seeking permission to deposit the $50,000 with the Court, allows the Court to figure out how to divide the funds and allow the insurance company to be released from further liability. The problem for you is that this interpleader process results delays the settlement of your personal injury claim at a time wherein you are already probably experiencing financial hardships from being off work. Like I said above, there is a way to protect yourself. Underinsured Motorist Coverage as discussed within.

---

[8] I will tell you below how to protect yourself from this kind of irresponsible driver.

The $10,000 refers to your insurance companies limit of responsibility for any damage you do for to the cars/property damage caused by the auto accident. So if you are driving a Harley-Davidson motorcycle worth $20,000, the insurance company for the at-fault driver is only responsible for $10,000 of your property damage. The only way to protect yourself in this instance is to put collision coverage on your own motorcycle insurance policy. Nevertheless, this area is not quite as important when you consider that you could be facing a $30,000 medical bill, for an accident that was not your fault.

In Kentucky, the statute for the state minimum amount of insurance coverage is contained in KRS 304.39-110. In Indiana, the statute is Indiana Code 9-25-4-5.

UNDERINSURED MOTORIST COVERAGE: PROCEDURAL ISSUES THAT MUST BE FOLLOWED!!!

Very simply, if you have personal injury claim stemming from a motor vehicle accident and you intend to collect underinsured motorist benefits, you have some procedural hoops that you must jump through to preserve this claim. In Kentucky, the relevant statute is KRS 304.39-320. In Indiana, the relevant statute is Indiana Code 27-7-5.

In essence, once you obtain a policy limits offer from the at-fault insurance carrier, you have to provide to the underinsured motorist carrier proof of that offer and proof of the limits of the at-fault driver's limits of insurance coverage before you can accept that offer. If you fail to do this and allow the underinsured motorist carrier a chance to preserve their right of subrogation against the at-fault driver, your claim for underinsured motorist benefits will be barred. I recommend you let an attorney handle this procedure rather than take a chance that you could mishandle it and jeopardize your underinsured motorist insurance claim. If you are going to handle an underinsured motorist claim on your own, make sure you follow the procedures laid out by the statutes to the letter.

UNINSURED AND UNDERINSURED MOTORIST COVERAGE: BUY IT! LOVE IT AND HOPE YOU WILL NEVER NEED IT!

When an at-fault driver does not carry any liability insurance on his motor vehicle, he puts more than just himself at risk. If the at-fault driver injures you, there will not be any automobile insurance to cover your damages. However, you may still have a personal injury claim from which we can recover monetary damages.

I look to your own auto or motorcycle insurance to see if you have uninsured motorist coverage. Similarly, if the at-fault driver has insurance but not enough to cover your compensatory damages, I can use your own auto insurance to recover underinsured motorist benefits once the policy limit for the at-fault drivers coverage has been exhausted.

UNINSURED MOTORIST COVERAGE: PROTECTING KENTUCKY AND INDIANA MOTORCYCLE WRECK VICTIMS

Uninsured Motorist Coverage protects you and your family when the automobile accident happens and the at-fault driver does not have any liability insurance on his or her automobile. While it is illegal to drive a car without insurance in most states, it is a common occurrence on Kentucky and Indiana roadways. I believe that it is something like one-third of all drivers don't carry insurance.

Assume that while driving home on a Saturday night you had a motorcycle wreck with a drunk driver. Now assume that the drunk driver did not pay the premium for his automobile insurance in a timely manner and was cancelled by his insurance company. While the drunk driver will most likely face criminal charges stemming from this automobile accident and his intoxication, the real question is what about the damages he has caused you because of this automobile-motorcycle wreck.

If the drunk driver did not pay his auto insurance premiums, it is very unlikely that he has any insurance coverage that might apply to this wreck. Consequently, how is he going to pay for your personal injury damages such as:

1) medical expenses;
2) your time off from work;
3) the property damage to your car;
4) your rental car;
5) and out-of-pocket expenses.

Yes, you can sue the drunk driver for all your compensatory and punitive damages![9] However, what good does it do you to obtain a judgment (basically a piece of paper that says you are owed money) if he has no money, assets or a home that can be used to pay for your personal injury damages. The key to preventing this type of situation is to have purchased **Uninsured Motorist Coverage** from your automobile insurance company or the company that insures your motorcycle.

Uninsured Motorist Coverage allows my client to recover their personal injury damages, stemming from a wreck, from his/her own insurance company. Your car insurance company, whether it be by a personal injury settlement or through a lawsuit, is responsible for the damages the drunk driver was legally responsible. Your insurance company will still argue with me about the extent of your medical and other damages, the reasonableness of your damages, the liability of the other driver and other items. However, uninsured motorist coverage provides a defined monetary source from which you can recover your damages. Without it, your only option is to sue the drunk driver, hope he has some assets and hope any judgment you obtain is not discharged when he files bankruptcy.

So in a motorcycle wreck wherein the at-fault driver has no insurance, the client can still recover his personal injury claim from his own insurance carrier. It is the client's insurance carrier who

---

[9] Punitive damages can be recovered when a driver is guilty of gross negligence or extreme recklessness. The argument is that a person's voluntary intoxication qualifies as gross negligence and therefore, justifies an aware of punitive damages. Punitive damages are harder to bankrupt than compensatory damages.

then sues the at-fault driver to try and recover what they paid out on your behalf. This way, your insurance company and not you, bears the risk that this at-fault driver has little to no money to pay for your damages.

I recommend that motorcyclists carry at least $100,000 of uninsured motorist coverage because for example, I have seen cases wherein the air ambulance bills alone total over $26,000.

CAN YOU REJECT YOUR UNINSURED MOTORIST COVERAGE?

Yes, legally your can reject this type of insurance coverage but, I would never, never, never recommend it!!! Instead, make sure you specifically ask for this insurance coverage and never sign anything wherein you are waiving this type of automobile insurance coverage. In short, if you don't have this insurance coverage, you may save yourself a couple of hundred dollars a year for a huge risk to you and your family. In the event of a serious motorcycle crash, you could owe thousands in medical bills, for an accident that was not your fault, just because you tried to save several hundred dollars.

On a side note, I pay for this extra insurance coverage by increasing the deductible on my automobile policies to $1,000 instead of $250. The idea being I can afford $1,000 much more than I can afford a $10,000 medical bill.

HOW MUCH UNINSURED MOTORIST COVERAGE DO I PURCHASE?

The amount of the coverage depends upon your financial needs and how much you can afford. I would suggest you discuss this issue with your insurance agent. However, I reasonably recommend that everyone carry at least $100,000 per person in uninsured motorist coverage. My reasoning being that if you do not have health insurance, this amount gives me the greatest chance of getting your medical bills paid should you be involved in a serious automobile accident. Recall that I am trying to make sure that you are protected when the car wreck results in surgery, loss of limbs or hospitalizations.

I WAS IN A MOTORCYCLE WRECK WITH AN UNINSURED MOTORIST, NOW WHAT DO I DO?

Call me at (502) 609-7657 or 855-REACHMYCELL. It is my job to make sure that the at-fault driver was truly uninsured. Don't assume that the other driver is truly uninsured for the following reason: 1) he might not have actually owned the vehicle; 2) he might have been working for an employer at the time of the car accident thereby putting the employer's coverage on the hook and; 3) had coverage through a policy in the household. *There are several ways in that someone can have insurance that may not be obvious.*

UNDERINSURED MOTORIST BENEFITS, PROTECTION AGAINST "Minimum Coverage for Minimum Budgets"

We have all heard the TV commercials wherein **SAFE AUTO INSURANCE COMPANY** advertises minimum insurance coverage for minimum budgets. However, do you really understand what this means?

Both Kentucky and Indiana law require that a car driver only carry insurance coverage in an amount of $25,000 per person and $50,000 per automobile accident. *THERE IS NO GUARANTEE THAT THE AT-FAULT DRIVER HAS INSURANCE COVERAGE TO PAY YOUR MEDICAL BILLS, LOST WAGES, OR YOUR CLAIM FOR PAIN AND SUFFERING.*

Let's assume that you and your spouse are riding your motorcycle on Interstate 64 when another driver crosses the center line and hits your bike head-on. The motorcycle accident is severe and you are both taken to the trauma center of the University of Louisville Hospital. You undergo surgery for several broken bones and are told you have a closed-head injury. Your spouse is treated and released. You are finally released from the hospital after 10 days and you are told you should not go back to work for four weeks. Further, when you open arrive home from the hospital and open the mailbox, you open a medical bill from U of L Hospital for $43,000.

In the upcoming weeks you receive several other bills from the emergency room doctors, the MRI provider, for a CT scan and from the X-ray physicians. In total, your bills come up to over $62,000. To date, your wife has incurred about $12,000 in medical expenses between the emergency room visit, an MRI and continuing chiropractic care. The problem is clear. If the at-fault driver is only insured to the extent required by Kentucky or Indiana law, **your medical bills alone exceed that insurance coverage**.

Kentucky and Indiana law allow a person to drive around with $25,000 in insurance, not enough to pay your medical expenses or the other aspects of your personal injury claim. Actually, in this example, your medical bills alone totaled over $62,000. Most insurance policies are sold in $25,000 increments until you get over $100,000 in coverage. As a result, in this example, the at-fault driver was probably underinsured even if he had $50,000 or $100,000 in insurance coverage.

The Solution: EVERYONE NEEDS TO MAKE SURE THEY HAVE UNDERINSURED MOTORIST COVERAGE ON EVERY AUTOMOBILE/MOTORCYCLE INSURANCE POLICY THEY HAVE.

Basically, underinsured motorist coverage transfers *THE RISK THAT THE AT-FAULT DRIVER DOES NOT HAVE ENOUGH INSURANCE COVERAGE TO YOUR OWN INSURANCE COMPANY*.

Underinsured Motorist Coverage allows me, as your lawyer, to make a claim on your behalf against the at-fault driver and your own insurance company. Basically, this coverage takes away the risk that the at-fault driver cannot fully pay your claim. It gives me a source from which I can recover, on your behalf, your medical bills, lost wages, future medical expenses and claim for pain and suffering.

Without Underinsured Motorist Coverage, you are **gambling** that the at-fault driver has enough coverage to pay your medical expenses, lost wages, pain and suffering and other damages. My recommendation is that every car or motorcycle owned by you or your business be insured for at least $100,000 of Underinsured Motorist Coverage per person. If you can afford more coverage, buy it!

WHAT DOES IT MEAN TO STACK INSURANCE COVERAGE?

Kentucky law allows stacking of uninsured and underinsured motorist benefits depending upon how the insurance policy is written. Indiana does not allow insurance policies to be stacked.

Simply put, stacking refers to recovering insurance polices from more than one applicable policy. By stacking coverage from more than one auto insurance policy — or coverage for more than one car on a single policy — the injured party can increase the total amount of his recovery, assuming the value of his claim is worth more than the just the initial insurance policy.

In other words, you own three vehicles: a Buick, a Toyota and a Ford Truck. On all three of these vehicles, you made sure you listened to my advice and put $100,000 of underinsured motorist coverage on each automobile policy. Well stacking means that since you effectively bought three $100,000 policies of underinsured motorist coverage, you have $300,000 of underinsured motorist benefits available to you even though you were only in one of your vehicles at the time of the accident.

Insurance companies generally do not like stacking policies and therefore, they have now written most of their insurance policies wherein a single policy of uninsured or underinsured motorist coverage will cover any vehicle you are in. So to use myself as an example again, I have two automobiles. However, I have one policy of underinsured motorist coverage. My insurance company specifically listed this coverage separate in my declarations page and wrote my insurance coverage in such a way that it would apply no matter which vehicle I am driving.

Now, let me explain to you how this concept applies to motorcycle riders. I had a gentlemen approach me about a case wherein his first medical bill was $22,000 and the at-fault driver was only insured for $25,000. I looked at the motorcycle policy and there was no underinsured motorist coverage. Nevertheless, we were able to get my client's underinsured motorist coverage from his automobile insurance to apply to the injuries he sustained while riding his motorcycle. Very simply, to avoid stacking, his insurance company wrote the underinsured coverage so that it would apply regardless of the vehicle he was operating. In this case, it meant we had an additional $25,000 in insurance coverage we could go after.

ERISA AND HEALTH PLANS: WE COULD WRITE AN ENCYLOPEDIA ON THE ISSUES.

To explain ERISA in a simple fashion, it is the law that governs the rights of health insurance carriers. If your medical bills were paid by health insurance of an employer's health plan, the insurance company or plan may want you to reimburse it out of any personal injury recovery. Your "insurance" turns out to be not insurance at all, but a "loan."

The gist of all ERISA law is that if they, the health plan, pay medical expenses on your behalf which were caused by someone's else's negligence and you recover a personal injury claim from any source, they have a right to recover from you. If this sounds intimidating, then I successfully conveyed my point.

The laws in some states, including Kentucky and Indiana, generally allow such claims by health insurance companies. Actually, ERISA law generally tries to claim that it is controlled by Federal Law and preempts state law.

This area of law, known as "reimbursement or subrogation" is actually quite complicated and is governed by a federal law called

ERISA (The Employee Retirement Income Security Act of 1974). Your attorney must understand the implications of ERISA on your case. In fact, this area is so complicated, I have utilized experts in the field to handle the ERISA portion of the case on an hourly basis when I have felt that their expertise would allow a greater reduction of the money the health plan was entitled to.

Almost every health insurance plan, whether it be private, Medicare, Medicaid or state-funded, has a provision in it that says they have a right to recover the medical bills they pay on your behalf if you recover on your personal injury claim. This right, anymore, is not limited to recoveries from third-parties but rather, includes recoveries made through uninsured motorist coverage, underinsured motorist coverage and no-fault benefits. Also, most health plans have contract language stating that they don't owe attorney fees on the amount they recover and that they are a first-priority lien that trumps your rights no matter how badly you are hurt.

The law regarding health plans is ever-changing. In fact, the U.S. Supreme Court issued another opinion that largely reaffirmed the superior, legal rights of health plans. For purposes of this book, I have to limit my discussion to say you need to understand that your health plan has a right to recover what they paid out in medical expenses as a result of your motorcycle accident. I know it is not fair and yes, I agree that they should not be allowed to recover anything since that is what we pay the health insurance premiums to cover. However, it's not matter if it is fair or not, is the law.

For my practice, I have to identify early on the interests of the health plan and look at their terms of the health insurance plan to determine the extent of their legal rights. Unfortunately, the health plan can come in and eat up much of a client's recovery. This is why I have to try and negotiate a reasonable settlement with them as every dollar that does not go into their pocket, goes into my client's pocket.

The bottom line is for those of you who are trying to handle a personal injury claim, make sure you address the interests of the health plan. The last thing you want to have happen is to settle your claim and get sued by your health plan several years after the settlement.

LIENS ON YOUR SETTLEMENT

A lien means that someone has a right to get paid back. If you have Medicare or Medicaid, they have a lien by statute. If you receive med-pay benefits, disability benefits or health insurance benefits, they have a lien by contract. Very simply, you have to assume that most companies these days have some kind of lien wherein they can recover whatever they paid on your behalf from your personal injury settlement. If you are going to try and resolve your personal injury claim on your own, make sure you address each and every lien that might exist as a result of this motorcycle accident.

"WHY SHOULD I LISTEN TO YOU?"

My name is James "Jim" Desmond and I have been representing individuals against insurance companies since 1999. I limit my practice to accident and injury cases; so, if you want a divorce or a will, or have a traffic ticket, I have to refer you to one of my friends. [10] You can find out more about me at my web site at www.attorneydesmond.com. Better yet, pick up the phone and talk to me directly!

People will ask me all the time why do I give out my cell phone to my clients. Why not? The biggest complaint against attorneys is not legal malpractice but lack of communication. You are my client. You are trusting me with some thing that affected your life and your family's lives. Why would I not want to hear from you!

> *Deal directly with me, Jim Desmond. Clients should be able to talk to their attorney and not have a paralegal or secretary as their only contact!*

I realize that a lawsuit may be the most important event going on in your life right now. Your case will be personally handled by me – not a paralegal.

I represent many people who have been injured by the negligence of others. I have also represented families of deceased loved ones in wrongful death cases. While each case is different, and past results cannot be used to predict future success, I can tell you that I have been privileged to help my clients and their families recover from the hardships their injuries have caused.

www.ingramcontent.com/pod-product-compliance
Lightning Source LLC
Chambersburg PA
CBHW021940170526
45157CB00005B/2363